◇

THE BEST MAN'S ORGANISER

by
Christopher Hobson

foulsham
LONDON • NEW YORK • TORONTO • SYDNEY

foulsham

Bennetts Close, Cippenham, Berkshire SL1 5AP

While every effort has been made to ensure the accuracy of all the information contained within this book, neither the author nor the publisher can be liable for any errors. In particular, since laws change from time to time, it is vital that each individual should check relevant legal details for themselves.

ISBN 0-572-02303-0

Copyright © 1993 and 1997 W. Foulsham & Co, Ltd

Printed in Great Britain by
Cox & Wyman Ltd, Reading, Berkshire

THE BEST MAN'S
ORGANISER

CONTENTS

INTRODUCTION

So you have been asked to be a best man at the wedding of your close friend or, perhaps, your brother. The chances are, you agreed with alacrity and said you would be delighted. You were probably a little flattered because it confirmed your long-standing friendship. But I wouldn't be at all surprised if you secretly feel something else as well - dread!

Isn't the best man supposed to be the organiser? He is the one who is level-headed, confident in a crisis, a born after-dinner speaker, a diplomat and a trouble-shooter all rolled into one. Isn't he? Doesn't sound much like you? Well, don't worry. If you were choosing a best man, you would not interview candidates and select the most suitable man for the job. You would want to ask your closest friend as a mark of your friendship and respect. So you are right to be flattered, because that is why you have been chosen.

But that still leaves the spectre of that best best man hovering at your shoulder. What are you going to do about him? Your friend has paid you the compliment of asking you to be his right-hand man on his special day, so you want to do a good job. Where are you going to find those marvellous qualities you will need to see you - and everyone

else - safely through the big day?

Relax. Someone who is born to be a superb best man is a rare commodity indeed; and yet people are doing a great job at it every day. And you have already taken the first step towards being a good best man by buying this book, because with a little foresight, preparation and planning, you can soon learn all the duties you will be expected to perform and how to carry them out to be the 'best man' (second to the groom, of course) on the day.

On rare occasions, there may be a female 'best man'. But since the best man is traditionally the groom's closest friend it is unlikely, even in these days of advancing equality, that this will happen often. The bride may have reason to think she should occupy that place, after all! There have been female 'best men' and there will be more, but since they will be only too aware of their own un-usual position, I am sure they will forgive the use of the male pronoun. All the information in this book is equally relevant to a 'best girl', except of course, for clothes. At a formal wedding a smart day dress with a corsage of fresh flowers would be appropriate. At a civil ceremony or second marriage, where the bride may wear a suit, the best girl could be similarly attired. Whatever you decide to wear, you will want to ensure that the bride wears more distinctive clothes than you, so that there is no confusion!

The important thing to remember, if you are asked to be best man, is that with some planning and preparation it will not be an ordeal, but a wonderful day to enjoy and celebrate with your friends. This book is full of useful tips and check-lists that will help to ensure that everything goes smoothly on the big day.

WHAT DO I HAVE TO DO?

Everyone knows that a best man is the groom's right-hand man and a general problem-solver and source of information on the wedding day. But what information is he supposed to have and what does he actually do? He does his best not to drop the ring down a grating in the church floor, of course, but there are a whole host of other responsibilities the best man undertakes which help to make the day run smoothly for the groom, and for everyone else.

This chapter will give you an outline of the main duties of the best man. Later chapters will give you all the detailed information you need on each subject, with personal checklists to help in your planning and preparation, and to ensure that you remember everything on the big day.

Before the event

The most important job of the best man is to help the groom. He should involve himself in the wedding preparations, help with choosing clothes and accessories, arranging cars, collecting the buttonholes and so on. He will probably help choose the ushers, explain their duties to them and make sure that they have the order-of-service sheets and buttonholes to distribute at the church. The best man will certainly play the major part in organising the stag party, and above all he must make sure that the groom is taken safely home to bed afterwards.

On the morning of the wedding

On the wedding day itself, the best man should keep the groom as calm as possible. Efficiently and without fuss, he must make sure that the groom is correctly dressed and arrives at the church on time with all the relevant documents, money and anything else he needs. Most important of all, the best man looks after the wedding ring until the moment it is required to seal the marriage.

At the church

Once at the church, the best man stays with the groom, and stands a little behind and to the right of him during the ceremony so that he can hand over the ring, or rings, at the appropriate moment. He escorts the chief bridesmaid into the vestry to sign the register, and escorts her out of the church at the end of the service. He should also be responsible for making sure the marriage fees are paid.

Outside the church, the best man helps the photographer to get everyone in the right place at the right time during the photographs, and then must ensure that everyone is safely dispatched to the reception after they have waved off the bride and groom.

At the reception

At a formal reception, the best man may be asked to announce the guests as they approach the receiving line. He can generally help to keep things running smoothly by offering drinks, chatting to guests, making introductions and helping people to their seats. He may introduce the first speaker, and he responds to the toast to the bridesmaids, gives a short speech of his own and reads the congratulatory telegrams. He dances with the chief bridesmaid, the bride, the bride and groom's mothers, and as many of the guests as possible.

Going away

The best man makes sure that the couple's car is all ready at the reception site to be driven away after the reception, packed with their luggage, all the necessary documents for their honeymoon, and beautifully decorated, too! He can help the bride's parents to see the guests safely on their way home, and perhaps give a hand with the clearing up.

Finally, he can sit down, put his feet up and enjoy a stiff drink with the chief bridesmaid and congratulate himself on a job well done!

THE QUALITIES OF A BEST MAN – AND HOW TO ACQUIRE THEM

Don't worry if you feel you lack some of the qualities you will need to see you successfully through the day; there are plenty of ways to acquire them. You may not be able to change your character completely, but with proper preparation anyone can be perfect for 24 hours!

Well-informed

During the run up to the wedding, and on the day itself, you will be called upon to play many different roles, answer a host of questions and solve a series of problems. To be ready for all this you must be well-informed. Make quite sure that you know the format for the day, what to expect, where to be at what time and what you are supposed to do.

If you are not an organised person, and think a 'filofax' is some new-fangled farm equipment, this is what you do. First, finish reading this book. Second, arrange a chat with the bride, groom and chief bridesmaid. Go through the arrangements with them, ask questions, and find out what the bride, in particular, expects. Finally, fill in all the checklists carefully as you go along so that you know everything will be ready and complete on time. Fill in the wedding day prompt cards at the back of the book to take with you. Then you can relax and enjoy yourself.

Level-headed

A dose of common sense will help you through most problems, should any arise on the day. If that is not your strong point, take a few sensible precautions. Take a step away from the grating when you take the ring from your pocket if you think you will drop it. Make sure you are well-informed and well-prepared, and be on good terms with the chief bridesmaid and the bride and groom's fathers to help you out if necessary. If you are in a jam, it can also help to think of the most sensible person you know, and try to imagine what they would do to solve the problem.

Punctual

Punctuality is important, especially since you are responsible for the groom's time keeping as well as your own.

If you are notorious at oversleeping, enlist a

neighbour to make sure you are up and about at the right time, or book an alarm call - or both. Time everything in advance, check roadworks and traffic conditions at the relevant time and day and make yourself a written schedule to follow. If you think even that will fail, again enlist some help. Ask your mother, or a friend to check with you at pre-arranged times that everything has been ticked off your list of things to do.

Sober

No one wants to stop you enjoying yourself, but to do a good job, you do need to be reasonably sober.

If knowing when to stop is not your strong point, take precautions. Taxis or lifts are essential for the stag party, but remember that you should still see the groom safely inside his house before you go home. On the wedding day itself, your speech will not be very well received if it is slurred, so have a word with the barman or waitress beforehand and ask them to serve you non-alcoholic drinks once you have reached your limit.

Observation and tact

As an all-round helper, observation and tact will come in handy, so that you can spot problems and keep everyone happy. A fixed grin won't fool anyone but try to keep smiling, listen, and watch what is going on around you.

If you find it difficult to anticipate problems,

try to imagine that you are three metres tall and can see everything going on beneath you. It will not only make it easier to single out the maiden aunt who is sitting on her own and would love to be asked to dance, it should bring a smile to your face.

A good speaker

The speech is probably the moment that the best man dreads the most. A good speech is important, but no one expects a polished, witty, professional performance.

Remember three things and it will seem much less daunting. First, that the speech should be no longer than four minutes at the outside - and that is a very small part of the whole day. Second, everyone in the room will be feeling warm and happy, and in no mood to criticise. Third, don't try to be someone you are not. Concentrate on being sincere and to the point. The best speeches are always the shortest ones; and with a little preparation and practice you can be certain of success.

How to prepare yourself

Now you have an idea of what is expected, you can get on to the detailed planning. The following chapters will work through every aspect of the planning and the wedding day itself. Read through the whole book once to absorb the full picture, then begin again when you are ready to start filling in details and actually making plans. The checklists will help you get through everything with the maximum efficiency.

In a nutshell, preparation is the key to acquiring all the qualities and performing all the duties of the perfect best man.

SETTING THE SCENE

The first and most important thing to do is so obvious that it is easily forgotten. Mark the date of the wedding in your diary (no matter how far in advance that may be), and cancel any other arrangements for that date, and preferably for the day before and the day after as well. Remember in particular regular sporting commitments, for example. If it is too early to make cancellations, mark a suitable date in your diary when you can inform the people involved.

Although, strictly speaking, you are 'employed' by the groom, in practice, the kingpin of any wedding - whether during the preparations or on the day - is the bride. The groom will have plenty to contribute to the planning and decision-making, but for most couples, the bride is the one whose ideas and preferences set the atmosphere for the day.

Naturally, every bride has her own ideas on how the day should be planned, the atmosphere she would like, and what she would like everyone to do; so the role of any best man will be slightly different in each case. It will also be affected by the

formality of the wedding; he will probably take a more prominent role in a formal wedding than an informal one, for example. The size of the bride's family may make a difference; if she has plenty of brothers and sisters to help with the organising, the best man may find that certain jobs are taken off his hands.

The important thing is not to make vague guesses as to what is required, but to find out as much as possible, well in advance, about what your role will entail. The details may change as the plans proceed, but that will not matter since you can soon make a few last-minute adjustments to your notes. What you want to avoid is finding out at the eleventh hour that the bride expects you to chauffeur the bridesmaids when you cannot drive, or that you are required in two places at once on the wedding morning. There are ways round any problem which may arise - if you plan ahead.

Meeting with the bride and groom

The simple solution is to arrange a meeting with the bride and groom, and also the chief bridesmaid if appropriate, about three months before the wedding. The bride and groom may arrange this for themselves, or you may meet them regularly anyway, but make sure that an evening is set aside to go through the plans and find out exactly what is expected. The chief bridesmaid will find it just as useful.

It will be an advantage if you have already read this book before the meeting. That way you will know the general duties you may be expected to perform and can concentrate on all the details of this particular wedding, and where you fit into the plans for it.

It is important, at this first meeting, to start at the beginning and work through everything that will happen on the wedding day: clothes for the groom and yourself, bearing in mind the colour schemes chosen for the bride and bridesmaids; ceremony time and venue; photograph details; transport arrangements to the reception; reception site and arrival time; numbers of guests; type of meal; timing of speeches; entertainment arrangements; bar facilities; time to leave. Fill in the wedding profile in Checklist 1 as you chat, and you will have a ready-made source of information to refer to as you go along. Some of the detailed information can be filled in or transferred to other checklists so that it is all to hand when you come to that part of the planning.

At this initial run through you will be able to establish the style of wedding, as well as the essential data. You will also be able to make sure you know what the bride expects you to do, whether there are any extra jobs which are not on your lists, special family customs and so on.

So, the first stage of your planning is complete - and was much easier than you expected! You have already experienced the confidence-boosting effect of having information at your fingertips, so you know how to proceed to the rest of the planning.

Checklist 1: WEDDING PROFILE

Date of Wedding _____

The wedding party

Bride's name _____
Address _____
_____

Telephone _____

Groom's name _____
Address _____
_____

Telephone _____

Chief bridesmaid's name _____
Address _____
_____

Telephone _____

Other bridesmaids' names, and ages (if children)
_____
_____
_____

Bride's parents' names _____
Address _____
_____

Telephone _____

Groom's parents' names _____
Address _____
_____

Telephone _____

Chief usher's name _____

Address _____

_____

Telephone _____

Usher's name _____

Address _____

_____

Telephone _____

Usher's name _____

Address _____

_____

Telephone _____

Clothes

Colour scheme for bride and bridesmaids _____

_____

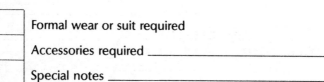

☐ Formal wear or suit required

☐ Accessories required _____

☐ Special notes _____

Transport

☐ Groom and best man to church _____

☐ Bridesmaids to reception _____

☐ Parents to reception _____

☐ Guests to reception _____

☐ Bride and groom for honeymoon_____

The ceremony

☐	Time _____
☐	Venue _____
☐	Name of minister/registrar _____
☐	Telephone _____
☐	Rehearsal date and time _____
☐	Arrival time for groom and best man _____
☐	Organ music; fees to organist _____
☐	Bells; fees to bell-ringers _____
☐	Order of service sheets _____
☐	Ushers' duties _____
☐	Buttonholes/corsages _____
☐	Photographs allowed in church _____
☐	Photograph arrangements _____
☐	Confetti allowed _____
☐	Parking facilities _____

The reception

☐	Time _____
☐	Venue _____
☐	Contact _____
☐	Telephone _____

The reception (continued)

☐
☐
☐
☐
☐
☐
☐
☐
☐
☐
☐
☐
☐
☐
☐

Parking facilities _____

Number of guests _____

Guests to be announced _____

Toastmaster _____

Receiving line _____

Seating plan _____

Meal arrangements and time _____

Bar facilities _____

Timing of speeches _____

People to thank in speech _____

Music/entertainment _____

Present display _____

Changing room for bride and groom _____

Leaving time _____

Departure details _____

Miscellaneous details

_____

_____

_____

MAKING PLANS

You will probably have several months in which to make your plans for the wedding, but if you have not been closely involved in any weddings before, you may be surprised how far in advance you should book clothes or catering services, for example, especially if the wedding is during the most popular summer months. So do not put off till tomorrow, what can be ticked off today. The checklist on page 32 will remind you what you should be doing and when.

Your invitation

Although you will probably be one of the first to receive a verbal invitation to the wedding, you will, traditionally, receive a formal invitation from the bride's parents about six weeks before the wedding. Don't assume that because they know you are coming, you need not reply. You should send a written reply immediately on receipt of the invitation. Address it to the bride's parents (or whoever sent the invitation). Most invitations are written in the third person, 'Mr and Mrs J. Jones request the pleasure of the company of . . . .'. If the arrangements are formal, you should reply in the same manner, although most people are happy to get an informal acceptance.

If you are married or engaged, naturally your wife or fiancée will be invited too. But if you do not have a regular partner, you should not bring along a total stranger, or someone you met only the week before. However, if the reception is to be an informal stand-up buffet, you might ask if she can come along to that.

Your gift

A wedding gift for the couple is important for any guest, and as their best man you will probably want to buy them a special present. Decide first whether you would rather buy them something practical for their new home, a touch of luxury, or perhaps something more personal. Then set the price limit so that you are not tempted to extravagance which you cannot really afford. It is much nicer to receive a thoughtfully chosen gift than one which you know is far too expensive.

Unless you have a clear idea of what the couple would like, it is usually best to ask to see the wedding list. If this has been well prepared, it will give you plenty of scope for a choice of gift in the style and price range you have selected. If the list is being managed by the bride, rather than a department store, it is very important to return it to her once you have made your choice. You could offer to hold a copy of the list yourself, in case you are asked for gift ideas by friends who would prefer not to ask the bride herself. Doing this can be very helpful, but only if you make certain to keep updating your list against the bride's master copy. Otherwise you could be responsible for embarrassing duplications.

Buy the gift, card and wrapping paper for your present well in advance, and remember to keep the receipt in a safe place just in case there are any problems, damage or duplicated gifts. Wrap it attractively, or if your packages look as though they have travelled round the world even before you give them, ask someone else to wrap it for you, then keep it in a safe place until just before the wedding. It is nicer to give them your gift before the actual day, perhaps at the rehearsal, since they will have so many other things to think about when the wedding finally arrives.

Helping the groom

The best man not only helps and supports the groom on the actual day of the wedding, he can also be invaluable during the planning stages as well. Make sure you keep up-to-date with what is happening, and see if there are ways in which you can help. You may be able to collect suits from the tailor, go with the groom to choose clothes or accessories, help with planning the honeymoon details or arranging documents and so on.

You can also act as a gentle reminder to make sure the groom gets everything done on time.

Remind him to check his passport, obtain travellers' cheques or inoculations, apply for licences or arrange for banns to be read, or even to buy the ring or a present for the bride.

Since the ways in which you can help out will vary from one wedding to another, the important thing is to be in touch and to offer your help so that the groom knows he can rely on you if necessary.

Helping the guests

Your main role as a supporter of the guests will be on the wedding day, but you may be called upon for advice as to a suitable wedding gift, help with booking a local hotel, information on routes or parking. Again, being well-informed and willing to help is the key to being most useful.

It is important to visit the reception venue, with the bride and groom, a couple of months before the wedding. Then you can have a look at the car park and check details with the hotel manager such as where the groom's car can be left, whether there is to be a toastmaster and the time by which all the guests must leave. The bride and groom will also need to book a room in which they can change into their going-away clothes.

Order-of-service sheets

Many brides have order-of-service sheets printed so that the guests can follow the service and hymns without referring back and forth from prayer book to hymn book. These should be collected in advance from the bride, and given to the chief usher. They will then be distributed by one of the ushers to the guests as they arrive at the church.

Buttonholes and corsages

By tradition, it is the groom who pays for the buttonholes for himself, the best man and ushers, so you may well get involved in flower arrangements. However, it will almost certainly be the bride who chooses the colour and type of flower. Normally, the principal men sport white carnations, and the bride's and groom's mothers have small corsages of flowers to match their outfits. These are usually delivered to the bride's parents' home on the morning of the wedding, along with the bouquets. Alternatively they may be delivered at the reception venue, with the table decorations, or you may need to collect them from the florist. It is important that whatever arrangement is made for getting the correct flowers to all those who need them, you, the bride and the florist must know exactly what it is. Normally it will be your responsibility, as best man, to ensure that you, the groom, the ushers and the groom's parents all have their flowers. The simplest way to achieve this is to collect the necessary flowers and distribute them at the church door. If you will be very pressed for time on the wedding morning, the whole matter could be delegated to a reliable usher - who should anyway reach the church before you.

Checklist 2: DIARY

6 months to go

Confirm acceptance with groom

Book wedding date in diary

Cancel any other arrangements

3 months to go

Discuss wedding plans with bride and groom

Help to choose the ushers

Help with the wedding preparations

2 months to go

 Consult the wedding gift list and decide on present

Arrange to pay for and fit your own outfit

Check that groom and ushers have organised their own outfits

 Prepare and draft speech

Practise and time speech

 Compile a list of close family

Give this list to ushers and instruct them on their duties and timing

Visit reception venue with bride and groom to check times, parking, etc.

Remind groom to check passports, order travellers' cheques and to have inocculations, etc.

6 weeks to go

 Organise stag party

Book venue for stag party

Check licence/banns arrangements have been made

1 month to go

 Check that buttonholes have been ordered

Check that honeymoon arrangements have been made

1 month to go (cont.)

☐ Check route to groom's home, to church and to the reception by doing test run(s)

☐ Arrange transport for groom and self to church, to reception and home

☐ Arrange going-away vehicle for newly-weds

☐ Arrange own transport from reception

☐ Arrange car service if appropriate

☐ Buy decorations for going-away car

2 weeks to go

☐ Finalise speech and write prompt card

☐ Check parking arrangements at church and reception

☐ Deputise ushers to assist with parking

1 week to go

☐ Attend rehearsal

☐ Fill in wedding day schedule

☐ Hand over gift to bride and groom

☐ Check ring is purchased (and carry a spare!)

☐ Check licence/banns certificate is collected

☐ Collect order of service sheets

☐ Ensure groom's safety at and after stag night

2 days to go

☐ Check and confirm transport arrangements

1 day to go

☐ Collect hired attire

☐ Check buttonholes

☐ Check car

☐ Ensure going-away luggage is packed

☐ Book an alarm call if necessary

☐ Make sure you have plenty of cash

WHAT TO WEAR

You will know the style of the wedding from your discussions with the bride and groom. For most weddings, there are two main options: either morning dress or a lounge suit. Whatever the bride has chosen, all the men in the wedding party - the groom, best man, bride's and groom's fathers and ushers - will wear the same style.

Morning dress

For most formal weddings, brides ask the men in the wedding party to wear grey morning suits. These comprise a grey suit with tail coat, grey top hat and gloves and usually a white shirt. It can be a plain shirt, a dress shirt, or one with a high winged collar worn with a cravat. Socks and shoes are generally black. A tie or cravat can be chosen to match the outfits, but should never be black. The bride may want you to select a colour to complement the bridesmaids' dresses and the flowers, in which case you should ask for a piece of fabric or a colour match. It is very difficult to remember a colour sufficiently well to match it, especially under the artificial lights of a shop. In any event, you should consult with the groom and choose something which looks compatible with his choice and does not outshine him.

Alternatively, the bride may choose a black tail coat and pinstripe trousers for the men. This is more likely for a winter wedding. Again, you would wear black shoes and socks, and a suitably matching tie or cravat, never black.

Morning suits are available in a range of colours, but if the bride gives you a free choice, she will probably expect that choice to be grey, so beware of choosing something unusual without consulting her and the groom. If you choose brown or maroon when everyone else is in grey, you will be the one to stand out rather than the groom - which would be very impolite - and the photographs will look extremely odd.

Although you will be carrying the hat and gloves most of the time and will only wear them for the photographs, they are an essential part of the morning dress. You should have them, and make sure you do not lose them.

Lounge suit

Many brides prefer a less formal approach, and ask the men in the wedding party to wear a suitable lounge suit. If you are not used to formal dress, this is probably the option you will prefer.

Even though there will be a range of styles and colours, you should take your cue from the groom so that your choice of outfits complements one another, and so that you do not outshine him. Choose a shirt and tie (never black), socks and shoes to match the suit.

It is equally important in an informal wedding as in a formal one to check on the colour scheme the bride has chosen for the bridesmaids and flowers, since if she is wearing a cream dress with bridesmaids in cream and rust, you and the groom may prefer brown suits rather than blue. Remember too, that the occasion will be one for celebration, so there is no need to be over-traditional. A nice bright tie and handkerchief will add a welcome splash of colour.

If the wedding is taking place in a registry office, a morning suit would look somewhat out of place, so follow the style of the groom, which will probably be a smart lounge suit.

Buying a suit

For a formal wedding, some people will buy a morning suit, but unless you attend formal occasions on a regular basis, this can be a waste of money as quality formal wear is very expensive. If you are wearing a lounge suit, however, you will almost certainly buy one for the occasion.

In either case, you should make sure that you know exactly what the bride would like you to wear and what the groom has chosen. It can be a good idea to shop together. If you rush out and purchase without consulting, it will be a big disappointment if you are asked to wear something else! Know the colour scheme, and think in advance about the type of suit you want. That will save time, and prevent you being distracted by unsuitable styles. Bear in mind that the suit will become part of your wardrobe, so think about a style which will be useful for your usual lifestyle.

Since the best man generally pays for his own clothes, you should also set your budget in advance, and remember that you will need shoes and other accessories as well as the suit itself. Browse around the shops and get an idea of what is available before you start to try on. Choose a suit which is comfortable, looks and feels good, and fits well. You and the groom can act as a useful second opinion for each other. Make sure that the trousers are the right length, and allow time to have them altered if they are too long or too short.

Complete your ensemble with matching shirt and accessories, so you have everything ready for the big day.

Hiring a suit

For anyone who would only wear a morning suit as a special favour to his best friend, hiring is the answer, and this includes most people in formal wedding parties.

If all the principal men are hiring their suits, the bride may arrange for you to visit the same shop and choose the style herself. Otherwise it will be up to you to choose a reputable firm and go along well in advance to try on and book your suit for the day. Again, it is a good idea to go along with the groom, and also the ushers so that you can all be fitted together and can select suitable ties or cravats etc. at the same time.

It is just as important that the suit fits well and is comfortable if you are hiring as if you are buying, so make sure that alterations to the trouser length, in particular, will be carried out before the wedding.

You will be asked to pay a deposit, to arrange a date and time for collection, final payment, and return. You can help the groom by collecting his suit along with your own, and you will almost certainly be responsible for returning it since he will be on his honeymoon.

Hair

The smartest suit will be spoilt if your hair is not well cut and groomed. Arrange for a hair cut about three weeks before the wedding, or a week before if you are absolutely sure no disasters will occur with the scissors.

Dress rehearsal

A quick dress rehearsal for yourself and the groom a week or so before the wedding (or as far in advance as possible if you are hiring) will not take long, and is a final check that you have both remembered everything. Make sure that new shirts have been taken out of the packaging and ironed, price tags have been removed from the soles of shoes, and everything feels and looks good together.

Checklist 3: YOUR CLOTHES

Style of clothes _____

Colour choice _____

Formal wear supplier _____

Address _____

_____

_____

_____

Telephone _____

Date for collection _____

Date for return _____

Hire deposit _____

Outstanding fee _____

Fee payable on _____

4 months to go

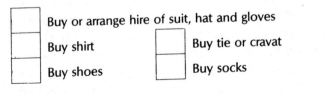

Buy or arrange hire of suit, hat and gloves

Buy shirt   Buy tie or cravat

Buy shoes   Buy socks

3 weeks to go

Make sure groom has wedding suit

Make sure ushers have wedding suits

Have hair cut

1 week to go

Collect suit (if hiring)

Dress rehearsal

CHOOSING THE USHERS

Traditionally, the best man is in charge of the ushers. He makes sure that they know their duties, are properly dressed in the same style as the groom and best man, and in the right place at the right time.

There are usually about four ushers, and traditionally the same number of ushers as bridesmaids. They are chosen by the groom, perhaps with help from the best man, and generally include brothers or close relatives of the bride and groom. It is a lot easier if the ushers have few other responsibilities of their own, so if the groom has a choice, guide him in the direction of those without small children to look after, or a long journey, for example. It may also be very helpful if they can drive, and better still have a car at their disposal. If the groom is worried about offending anyone, he should explain the situation to them; they are sure to understand.

Briefing

It creates a much more friendly and relaxed atmosphere on the wedding day if the principal men have met; so arrange a drink with the groom and the ushers a couple of months before the wedding, especially if you have not met them before. You will probably meet them again at the stag night, but that is not the time for talking about wedding details.

Make sure they know what type of suit they will be expected to wear, and where to hire it if necessary. They should also plan what shoes and other accessories they will need. Remind them to book a hair cut about three weeks before the wedding.

Go through their duties with them, and explain what will be expected of them on the day.

The chief usher should take charge of the buttonholes and order-of-service sheets at the church, either collecting them from the bride or from you prior to the ceremony.

At the church

The ushers should be the first to arrive at the church, about an hour before the ceremony. They distribute the buttonholes and corsages to the principal guests and direct all the guests to their correct places. They should also politely request anyone carrying confetti to keep it for the reception if the minister does not allow it to be thrown in the church grounds, and if photographs are not allowed inside the church, any guest carrying a camera should be discreetly warned. It may be useful if one usher organises car parking and if it is raining he should be armed with a large black umbrella.

Seating arrangements

As the guests arrive, one usher hands each an order-of-service sheet or hymn and prayer book and asks if they are friends of the bride or the groom. At a formal occasion, another would offer his arm to a lady, and escort her to a seat on the left-hand side of the church if she is a guest of the bride, and the right-hand side of the church if a guest of the groom. Her partner or any children would follow behind. If two single ladies arrive together, then the usher would escort the eldest first, and the other would wait for him to return, or for another escort. At a less formal wedding, the ushers should simply direct the guests to their seats, bride's friends on the left, groom's on the right. If the numbers of guests on each side of the church are clearly unbalanced, the ushers can use their discretion in filling the seats, though this is a matter you might be wise to check with the bride and groom beforehand.

The groom's parents sit in the second pew from the front on the right hand side. If there are any divorced parents in the family, you should warn the ushers, and explain the relevant seating arrangements. Normally, if either the bride's or groom's parents are divorced but not remarried, they would be seated together as usual. If they are divorced and remarried, the mother would sit in the first pew with her husband, and the father in the next pew with his wife. The last guest to arrive is the bride's mother, who should be escorted to her seat by the chief usher. She will sit in the front pew on the left of the aisle, leaving one spare seat on her right for her husband to take when he has 'given away' the bride. The ushers should set themselves near the back of the church so that they are in a convenient position to deal with any late-comers.

Seating plan

It's not a bad idea to visit the church when no wedding or service is taking place so that you can draw up a seating plan, filling in the names or status of guests.

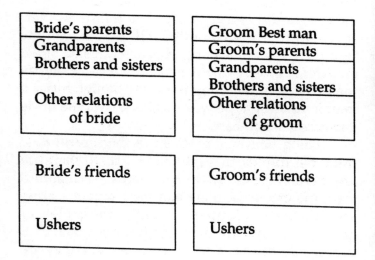

After the ceremony

After the ceremony, the ushers can be generally useful in helping to move people to the right place for the photographs, arranging transport, and directing people to the reception venue. The chief usher should check round the church to make sure that no one has left anything, particularly toppers and grey gloves.

The reason that there were traditionally the same number of ushers and bridesmaids is that they are supposed to provide escorts for the bridesmaids during the course of the day. Since escorts are no longer considered essential, this particular duty is not always strictly followed, but it is thoughtful if they can ensure that the bridesmaids are looked after during the day.

At the reception

At the reception, the ushers may be asked to help in offering drinks to guests as they arrive, introducing people to one another, and dancing with as many partners as possible.

Being an usher is not a great responsibility, but if the job is done well, it helps the wedding day go smoothly, and takes several minor worries from those principally involved in the celebrations.

Checklist 4: USHERS' DUTIES

Chief Usher _____

Address _____

_____

Telephone _____

Usher 1 _____

Usher 2 _____

Usher 3 _____

2 months to go

☐ Meeting with best man and groom

☐ Buy or hire suits, gloves and hats

1 month to go

☐ Have hair cuts

☐ Briefing on duties

☐ Confirm arrival time at church

1 week to go

☐ Collect order-of-service sheets from best man

The day

- [ ] Collect and distribute buttonholes
- [ ] Distribute order-of-service sheets
- [ ] Escort or direct guests to their seats
- [ ] Escort bride's mother to her seat
- [ ] Assist with parking at the church
- [ ] Help with photographs
- [ ] Assist in arranging transport to the reception
- [ ] Check that nothing has been left in the church
- [ ] Assist with parking at the reception
- [ ] Escort bridesmaids
- [ ] Serve drinks as guests arrive at the reception
- [ ] Help guests to enjoy the reception

To The Church On Time

'**G**et me to the church on time!' is the request of a groom to his best man, and has to be one of your most important duties on the wedding day.

The bride, the wedding party and the guests organise their own transport to the church, so unless you are asked to help out in a particular case, your only concern is how you and the groom arrive at the church, and how the happy couple will leave for their honeymoon. It is helpful if you can check with the bride whether anyone will need a lift from the station to the church, for example, so that you can arrange this, but it is not an essential duty.

The ushers should be at the church about an hour before the wedding, so make sure they have made suitable transport arrangements. Warn them about any parking problems, and if parking is difficult, arrange for one of them to supervise outside the church.

Using your own car

If you are taking your own car, check beforehand that it has been serviced and is in good working order. Check the oil and water, give it a thorough clean inside and out and fill up with petrol the day before.

Hired car

If you are hiring a car, book well in advance and double-check the arrangements a day or so before the wedding. Know exactly when the car is being delivered, or when you should collect it, check that it will be clean, that the tank will be full of petrol, and make sure you know about all the charges you will be expected to pay and when the car has to be returned.

Test runs

Double-check the time it will take you to drive to the groom's house so you know exactly when to set out. You should arrive at the church at least 15 minutes before the ceremony, and you and the groom will be far more comfortable if you aim for half an hour. Do a couple of test runs before the day, at the right time and on the relevant day of the week, so that you know the route well, and exactly how long it takes to get from home to the church. It is very risky to just make a guess, especially if you do not know the road well, or if you are used to driving along it at a different time of day or a different day of the week. Time the route, check the traffic conditions, and anything unusual such as roadworks. Find out about any special events on the wedding day itself. You will be in big trouble with the bride if you find that the road is closed for a carnival procession right at the critical time! Also check on the parking arrangements at the church so there is no danger of having to go round the block ten times trying to park. Fill in all the information on your checklists.

Emergencies

Just in case the unthinkable happens and the car will not start as you are about to set off, or breaks down en route, have a few telephone numbers of taxi firms to hand. Ring them up in advance and find out how long you would generally expect to wait for a taxi at that time - some firms may be able to offer a quicker service than others. Buy a phonecard, and have some change in your pocket for emergency calls.

From church to reception

Once you are safely at the church and with the ceremony over, you and the ushers should play a large part in getting everyone to the reception. The bride and groom will leave in the wedding car, followed usually by the wedding party - the bridesmaids, the bride's and groom's parents. The bride may have arranged additional wedding cars for the wedding party, or she may ask you to drive the bridesmaids while the two sets of parents drive their own cars. Know in advance whether you are taking any of the wedding party to the reception. If you are, you may like to have bought ribbons for your car.

Check with the bride beforehand whether any guests will need transport arranged for them, and work this out before the day if possible. You may be able to arrange for some of the ushers to act as chauffeurs, or ask guests with room in their cars to give a lift to other guests. Do as much as possible before the day, and make sure drivers and passengers know what is expected.

Either you or one of the ushers should go quickly on to the reception to help with parking there.

After the reception

After the reception, the bride and groom will be leaving for their honeymoon. If they are to leave in a taxi or hired car, you should make sure that it is booked at least a couple of weeks before the wedding, and confirm the booking two days before. If the groom will be using his own car, it is up to you to make sure that it is safely parked at the reception venue, already filled up with petrol and ready to go. You can do this the day before, or on the morning of the wedding. Either way, make sure you have transport back from the reception venue after you have left the groom's car there! The couple's cases can be left in the boot, or taken to the reception venue and loaded at the last minute.

It is usually the best man who organises a group of the younger guests to decorate the car, but do make sure that no one tampers with the mechanics of the car, or uses anything which may damage the paintwork. It would be really thoughtful to pack a small cleaning-up kit in the boot too, so that the bride and groom can stop to clean up the car if necessary. Include some rags , a wet sponge in a plastic bag, some scissors (if you have tied anything to the bumper) and some moistened wipes and kitchen roll to clean themselves up as well!

Lastly, make sure you know what time the happy couple want to take their leave, so that you can bring their car to the main entrance at the right moment.

Checklist 5: TRANSPORT

4 weeks to go

- Arrange for hire car if needed
- Have own car serviced
- Check groom's car has been serviced
- Buy ribbons if wanted
- Check route to groom's home at right time and on right day
- Check route to church at right time and on right day
- Check roadworks, special events, etc.

- Order taxi for you and groom to church if you are not driving

2 weeks to go

- [ ] Check parking arrangements at the church
- [ ] Check that ushers have transport to church
- [ ] Check with bride whether special arrangements are needed for any guests to be taken to reception
- [ ] Book taxi to get back from leaving groom's car at reception venue
- [ ] Book taxi to collect bride and groom from reception if needed
- [ ] Buy a phonecard
- [ ] Check parking arrangments at the reception
- [ ] Deputise ushers to assist with parking at church or reception if necessary

1 day to go

- [ ] Clean car
- [ ] Fill up with petrol
- [ ] Make sure groom's car is filled with petrol and parked at reception venue
- [ ] Arrange items for decorating going-away car
- [ ] Pack cleaning-up kit in groom's car
- [ ] Make sure bride's and groom's luggage is packed

The day

Tie ribbons on your car

Time to leave for ceremony _____

Arrival time at church _____

Departure time from reception _____

Car hire firm _____

Address _____

_____

Telephone _____

Car to be supplied _____

Date and time for collection/delivery _____

Taxi firm _____

Address _____

_____

Telephone _____

Taxi firm _____

Address _____

_____

Telephone _____

THE BEST MAN'S SPEECH

This is the part that most people dread the most, but with a little planning and preparation it really need not be as terrifying as you think. Very few people are practised 'after-dinner' speakers, and your audience does not expect a slick, professional performance. They simply expect the groom's friend to say a few sincere and perhaps amusing words and get on with the toasts so that they can really enjoy themselves!

Do I have to give a speech?

The answer to this question is almost certainly 'Yes'. Even at a very informal wedding, there are always toasts to the bride and groom and the bridesmaids, and some telegrams to read out, so you will be expected to say something. However, a best man's speech should only be about four minutes long at the most, so do not worry unduly about finding enough to say.

The speeches

When there is a sit down meal, the speeches and toasts generally happen after the last course, so that the cake can be cut and served with the coffee. In the case of a buffet reception, the cake will be cut and the speeches made once the bride and groom have had time to greet all their guests. However, to be quite certain of the timing you should check with the bride as to what arrangements she would prefer.

The sequence is very simple. Someone acts as a toastmaster to introduce the speakers. In most cases this is the best man, although at a formal wedding there may be a professional toastmaster. At the appropriate moment, you should stand and ask for silence. Give the guests a few minutes to quieten down, never just continue over a hubbub of voices. You should then introduce the father of the bride and take your seat.

The bride's father
The bride's father will thank everyone for coming to the wedding and welcome his new son-in-law into the family. His speech may be livened up with a few anecdotes about his daughter as a child or the time he first met the groom. He then proposes the toast to the bride and groom. Everyone stands to drink the toast, then sits down to listen to the groom.

The groom
The groom thanks his new father-in-law for his daughter's hand and his toast, and the guests for their good wishes and presents. He then makes a few complimentary remarks about the bridesmaids and proposes the toast to them.

The best man

Then it is the turn of the best man. He thanks the groom on behalf of the bridesmaids, and generally adds a few complimentary remarks of his own. He may thank anyone who has helped him to do his job properly, or the bride may ask him to thank someone on her behalf. Then he will congratulate the bride and groom, and add a story about how the couple first met or some suitable amusing anecdote, and finally read the telegrams. It is up to the best man to omit any telegram which might be unsuitable in the presence of young children and maiden aunts!

If the bride has chosen to say a few words, the best man should introduce her at this point. Check this beforehand, since it is up to the bride whether she chooses to speak. Finally, the bride and groom will cut the cake. Once the cake is cut, the waitresses may either serve coffee, or it may be the signal for people to leave the tables and circulate, or for the bride and groom to start the dancing.

How to write a speech

Unless you are an extremely accomplished speaker, you should plan your speech out in advance. It is not a good idea to write it out and read it, since this will not come over well and will put your audience to sleep. Similarly, if you write it out and memorise it, it is very inflexible, and does not allow you to extemporise or add your comments on what has happened during the day. The best way is to work out a speech which has shape and includes all the main points which you should not forget. Write out some notes on the Wedding Day Prompt Card, including names or particular things you want to mention. Then you have all the information you need, but you can add amusing comments or develop the material as best suits the occasion.

Start with a large sheet of paper, and write down everything you must include - thanking the groom for the toast to the bridesmaids, congratulations to the happy couple, and so on. Then think about what you would like to say, perhaps recall an incident about the couple which would make an amusing story. How did the couple meet, for example? Is there a story there? Note down some of the achievements in the bridegroom's life - sporting, academic or career. All these things are possible ideas for your speech, and once you have jotted them down you can arrange them into beginning, middle and end.

The beginning

The beginning of your speech should capture the audience's attention and be light-hearted and amusing. It will probably deal with the bride and groom's triumphs, achievements and antics. You might start with how long you have known the groom:

'I have known (the groom) for (a very long time), and though I have not had the pleasure of knowing the bride for so long, I am sure they will be very happy together. My only regret is that I did not meet (the bride) first . . .'

Never start your speech with 'Unaccustomed as I am to public speaking . . .' Unless, that is, you want everyone to groan!

The middle
Here you could include an amusing anecdote about how the couple met; suggest the changes that are likely to take place in their lifestyle; or warn the bride about her new husband's bachelor habits. You might have an amusing tale to tell about getting the groom home after the stag night; or to the church on time.

The end
This should contain a message of hope and congratulations for the future of the happy couple. Thank the groom for his toast to the bridesmaids, and add a few complimentary remarks of your own about them:

'You have only to look at the bridesmaids to understand why I was happy to accept the duties of best man . . .'

It is usual to conclude with a toast to the parents of the bride, and possibly to the parents of the groom, particularly if they have shared the wedding costs, or if the majority of the guests are their relatives and friends.

What to avoid
It is not good form to do any of the following:
1. Mention previous girlfriends or anything the least bit dubious in the groom's past.

2. Mention past marriages or relationships.
3. Speak for longer than four minutes.
4. Use unnecessarily long words or sentences.
5. Use formal words or phrases that you would not normally use.
6. Tell lies.
7. Put on an accent.
8. Be pompous or patronising.
9. Use slang.
10. Tell 'in' jokes which not all the audience will understand.
11. Swear or blaspheme.
12. Tell risqué jokes.
13. Make fun of anyone unkindly, except yourself.
14. Refer to the honeymoon or future children.

Quotations

If you feel it would help to give your speech a purpose, you can use a quotation to give it shape. Never use more than one, and only drop it in as the source of an idea, not to show off your literary knowledge. If everyone knows that you burned your library ticket ten years before, you can even laugh at yourself for having had to search through books for something suitable.

On the following page are a few quotations you may like to consider for your speech. Remember, though, that they should be used as an introduction to a story or an idea, not just for the sake of it. Many writers did not have too high an opinion of marriage, so make sure you choose something which will not offend.

'It is a truth universally acknowledged, that a single man in possession of a good fortune, must be in want of a wife.'

'Next to being married, a girl likes to be crossed in love a little now and then.' JANE AUSTEN

'Wives are young men's mistresses; companions for middle age; and old men's nurses.'

FRANCIS BACON

'Being a husband is a whole-time job. That is why so many husbands fail. They cannot give their entire attention to it.' ARNOLD BENNETT

'I am not against hasty marriages, where a mutual flame is fanned by an adequate income.'

WILKIE COLLINS

'When you're a married man, Samivel, you'll understand a good many things as you don't understand now; but vether it's worth while going through so much to learn so little, as the charity boy said ven he got to the end of the alphabet, is a matter o'taste.' (*Pickwick Papers*)

CHARLES DICKENS

'Every woman should marry, and no man.'

BENJAMIN DISRAELI

'Love and scandal are the best sweeteners of tea.'

HENRY FIELDING

'I chose my wife, as she did her wedding gown, not for a fine glossy surface, but such qualities as would wear well'.   OLIVER GOLDSMITH

'A gentleman who had been very unhappy in marriage, married immediately after his wife died: Johnson said, it was the "triumph of hope over experience".'

'Marriage has many pains, but celibacy has no pleasures.'   DR SAMUEL JOHNSON

'Marriage is a wonderful institution, but who wants to live in an institution?'   GROUCHO MARX

'Marriage is like a cage; one sees the birds outside desperate to get in, and those inside equally desperate to get out.'   MICHEL DE MONTAIGNE

'Strange to say what delight we married people have to see these poor fools decoyed into our condition.'   SAMUEL PEPYS

'Nothing is to me more distasteful than that entire complacency and satisfaction which beam in the countenances of a new-married couple.'

'Boys are capital fellows in their own way, among their mates; but they are unwholesome companions for grown people.'

'Marriage is nothing but a civil contract.'
JOHN SELDEN

'But love is blind, and lovers cannot see The pretty follies that themselves commit'

(Merchant of Venice)

'The world must be peopled. When I said I would die a bachelor, I did not think I should live till I were married.' *(Much Ado About Nothing)*
WILLIAM SHAKESPEARE

'It is women's business to get married as soon as possible, and a man's to keep unmarried as long as he can.'

'Marriage is popular because it combines the maximum of temptation with the maximum of opportunity.'

G. BERNARD SHAW

'All for love, and nothing for reward.'
EDMUND SPENSER

'Marriage is a sort of friendship recognised by the police'.

'No woman should marry a teetotaller.'

'In marriage, a man becomes slack and selfish, and undergoes a fatty degeneration of his moral being.'

'Marriage is like life in this - that it is a field of battle, and not a bed of roses.'

'To marry is to domesticate the Recording Angel.

Once you are married, there is nothing left for you, not even suicide, but to be good.'

ROBERT LOUIS STEVENSON

'Some respite to husbands the weather may send. But housewives' affairs have never an end.'

IVAN TURGENEV

Jokes

Let's face it, either you are good at telling jokes or you are not. If not, taking a joke from a book could be a big mistake, because the chances are you will forget the punchline or not tell it well enough to make people laugh. And nothing will fall flatter than a joke which no one understands or thinks is funny.

If you are good at telling jokes, bear in mind that you might want to use one, and store in your memory or make a note of any particularly apt jokes which you hear in the months before the wedding. Funny stories or anecdotes tend to be the easiest ones to fit into a speech. Try to make it flow fairly naturally into your speech; don't just slot a joke in for its own sake since it will sound out of place. Try it out on a family audience, too, to see how they react. Remember that anything 'blue' or in any way dubious or offensive is definitely out. If you are likely to be telling the same joke after 11 p.m. at the stag night, then it should not be in your speech!

PRACTISING THE SPEECH

You will probably make several draft sets of notes until it shapes up into a reasonable speech. Once you are happy, write out a draft notecard and practise your speech aloud in front of a mirror. It will give you lots more confidence, and will also allow you to hear how well the items run together. Sometimes a link which appears logical on paper, does not work when it is spoken. Time yourself; the speech should be no longer than four minutes. Remember to breathe while you are talking! It may sound obvious, but if you are nervous, you may tend to hold your breath without realising it, and a few practice runs will enable you to relax a bit more.

Presentation

Watching yourself in the mirror will also help you to present the speech well. These guidelines should also be useful.

First, remember that there will always be a babble of comments between speeches as well as scraping of chairs and fidgeting as people get comfortable. Don't compete with this, just wait until the room is reasonably quiet. Use the time to take a few relaxing deep breaths, glance through your notes and get yourself ready.

Stand comfortably, and don't shuffle your feet or fiddle with your nails, clink the change in your pocket or keep putting your hands in and out of your pockets. Decide beforehand how you are going to stand and what you will do with your hands. They can be a problem if you are nervous, but you can always hold your notecard, or take a tip from the Royals and hold them behind your back. Only make gestures to illustrate your speech if this comes naturally, otherwise they will look posed and peculiar.

Speak clearly and a little louder than normal, but don't shout and don't rush. Keep the tone conversational, as though you were talking to friends - which you are! The audience is not there to be critical, but to share a celebration with you. Look at them as you speak, but not with a fixed stare, let your eyes gaze around, and look at people when you refer to them, or propose a toast. This will help you to pitch your speech to the audience.

Stick to the plan you have made and don't waffle, but be flexible if you think of something amusing to add. Keep it short and to the point, be sincere, and remember to breathe!

The telegrams

This should be simple once your speech is over. Try to glance over the telegrams beforehand so that you can weed out anything unsuitable. If there are too many, select a few otherwise you will bore the guests reading out 'Best Wishes' over and over again from people they have never heard of. Check with the bride in case there are any which she would definitely like included. Read the message clearly, and take a deep breath between each one which will allow time for everyone to mutter 'Oh, how nice!' or 'Oh. John and Mabel, I haven't seen them for years!'.

Checklist 6:
PLANNING YOUR SPEECH

2 months to go

☐ Prepare draft speech

☐ Check with bride if specific people are to be mentioned

☐ Practise speech

☐ Time speech

☐ Decide how you will stand/what you will do with your hands

2 weeks to go

☐ Finalise speech

☐ Write prompt card

Speech ideas

Anecdotes about bride and groom _____

_____

_____

Quotation/story/joke _____

_____

_____

Thank groom for toast and compliments to bridesmaids

_____

_____

Own compliments _____

_____

Particular notes of thanks to _____

_____

Conclusion _____

_____

Telegrams/telemessages _____

_____

THE STAG PARTY

The stag party must be the least arduous duty for any best man! His job is simply to organise the celebration for the groom, enjoy the evening, and make sure everyone gets home safely.

It used to be traditional for the groom to celebrate the very last night of his bachelorhood, but it is far more sensible to hold the party a few days before, or even the weekend before the wedding. Then you don't have to worry about getting up the next morning.

Guests

Chat with the groom about the friends he would like to invite. He may issue the invitations himself, or he may ask you to arange matters, but it is usually done informally when you see friends, or by telephone. The ushers usually attend, as well as the bride's and groom's brothers and close friends of the groom. Traditionally both the bride's and groom's fathers are invited but leave early.

Venue

It is up to the groom how he would prefer to spend the evening. The most popular format is an inexpensive meal followed by a trip to the pub - or pubs. Remember to book a table in advance if you want to have a meal, especially if there is to be a large group of you.

Who pays?

Traditionally the groom pays for the stag party, but with current prices, it is more likely that the guests will pay at least some of the cost. For example, the groom may pay for the meal and the guests put into a kitty for the drinks, or vice versa. Let the guests know what they will be expected to pay for to avoid any embarrassment on the night. You should take charge of the money and make sure there is enough. Have some spare cash of your own handy just in case.

The best man's speech

Obviously you will want to enjoy yourself and have a few drinks, but try not to lose all self control! Use the occasion to test your speech-making skills, but don't forget that the jokes you test on the stag party audience will almost certainly not be suitable for the wedding itself.

The speech should be humorous, poking as much fun as possible at the groom. Some of the points you might include are:

1.　Amusing anecdotes from the groom's school or university days - particularly if you have known him for a long time.

2. Reference to the unfortunate girls who are now going to be abandoned by the groom – and the problem of getting rid of them.
3. Comments about carefree bachelor days being over; now he will be under his bride's thumb; having to mend his ways, etc.
4. Suggestions as to how he might still escape his fate.

Transport

Make transport arrangements before the event since on no account should anyone be allowed to drive. Either walk, or arrange to be collected by a taxi and driven home. Make sure the other guests have made suitable arrangements, or book taxis to 'bus' you all home. Have the addresses of the guests who are going home in each taxi clearly listed on sheets of paper so there is no confusion with the taxi driver.

Even if you arrange a taxi, you should remain sufficiently sober to see the groom safely inside his house before you go home.

Checklist 7: BOOKINGS REMINDER

4 weeks to go

☐ Arrange date for party

☐ Invite guests

☐ Book table for meal

1 week to go

☐ Book taxis

☐ Write out addresses for taxi drivers

On the night

☐ Take sufficient money

Taxi firm _____

Address _____

Telephone _____

Taxis booked from _____

To collect guests from _____

Restaurant _____

Address _____

Telephone _____

Time table booked _____ Number of people _____

THE REHEARSAL

Before many weddings, there is a rehearsal at the church a week or so before the event. This is an excellent chance for as many of the wedding party as possible to get together to check what will happen on the day, and make any last minute adjustments to arrangements.

Rehearsal dinner

Sometimes the bride and groom arrange a small dinner or other celebration for the wedding party after the rehearsal, to thank them for their support. This is a suitable time to present the couple with your wedding gift, so that they can unwrap it at leisure.

Final arrangements

Use the rehearsal as a chance to check on the arrangements, get to know the close members of both families, and ask any outstanding questions. You may want to finalise arrangements for collecting buttonholes or order of service sheets, check on lifts for guests from the church to the reception, parking, numbers of guests, times and so on. You can also take this opportunity to make sure that you know the names and faces of the close members of both families, and discover distinguishing features of any who cannot get to the rehearsal. Commit this information to memory and you will do a far better job when it comes to the big group photograph and introductions at the reception. Going through everything in detail at the rehearsal will be time very well spent and may save you from some frantic moments later on.

Checklist 8: REHEARSAL DETAILS

Date _____

Time _____

Venue _____

Questions for the bride _____

_____

_____

_____

_____

_____

_____

_____

_____

_____

_____

_____

Names not to be forgotten _____

_____

_____

_____

THE MORNING OF THE WEDDING

The morning of the wedding will be quite a busy time for you, and there are plenty of things which cannot be done further in advance but which you will not want to forget. The way to make sure that the day goes smoothly is first to know what has to be done, by reading all the information in these pages and double-checking with the bride and groom. Then you should get as many tasks as possible out of the way before the wedding day itself.

Then, a week or so before the ceremony, you can finalise your personal schedule and checklist for the day so that nothing is missed out and there are no last-minute panics because something takes longer than you thought it would. The schedule is just as important as the checklist because, provided you make it realistic, it will tell you whether you will make it to the church on time. On the day, check regularly against the schedule to be sure that all is well.

A few days before the wedding, you can go through the list, completing any jobs which can be done in advance. This will minimise the rush on the day and help to calm your nerves.

Make sure you get to bed early the night before the wedding, having set your alarm or arranged an alarm call, or asked a reliable friend to drag you bodily out of bed at the right time if you are really dreadful at getting up.

Phone calls

The groom
Make sure that the groom is up and about, has all his clothes ready and is going to have a proper breakfast! Check that he has all the documents and other things he will need: the rings; the certificate of banns from his church or the marriage licence; money for church fees; passport, tickets and other vital documents; case packed for honeymoon; car keys if his car has already been left at reception site; any telegrams that have arrived at his address. If his car is to be parked at the reception site this morning, ready for the couple's getaway, remind him what time you will arrive to drive it there, and make sure he has put the honeymoon cases and going away clothes inside it. Lastly, remind him of the time you will be returning to collect him for the ceremony. Then ring to confirm the taxi to take you back home.

The ushers
Confirm with the ushers the time they should arrive at the church; that they know the correct location; and have all their clothes and cars ready. Make sure the chief usher has the order-of-service

sheets ready to take with him. You should have either delivered these to him beforehand, or made sure that he collected them from the bride. Check that he has arranged to collect the buttonholes from the bride, florist or reception venue if you are not doing this job yourself.

The bride

Wish the bride and her parents well, and make sure there are no last-minute hitches which you could help to solve. Remind the bride's father to bring any telegrams to the reception, and check that the bride's honeymoon cases and going away outfit are safely at the reception venue.

Don't forget to eat!

Have a good breakfast, and make arrangements for lunch. Especially if the wedding is in the early afternoon, you may find that time for eating is absorbed in getting ready, but you should eat something; no one wants a best man who faints from hunger during the ceremony. So if you will not have much time for lunch, pack up a few sandwiches, fruit and so on and find time to eat.

Final checks

Use the list to tick off each item as you check it.
Check over your car, making sure that it is full of petrol, running well and clean inside and out. Tie on the wedding ribbons.

Check over your clothes, and go through the things you will need to take with you: phonecard; change for the telephone; taxi firm numbers; prompt cards; a spare ring just in case of disasters (a curtain ring or any cheap substitute will do); handkerchiefs (if you don't use them, someone will have forgotten theirs); money; things to decorate the going-away car; cleaning kit to pack in the groom's car; a couple of umbrellas just in case. Pack all your essentials in a bag, and make sure your suit is covered with a plastic cover.

Collect the groom

Set out for the groom's house in plenty of time, taking your clothes and essentials with you, so that you can dress at the groom's house. Once you are dressed and ready, double-check that neither of you have left the price tags on your shoes, and make sure you have everything you need. Take the rings and put them in a safe pocket, and take the money to pay the church fees, and any other documents, from the groom. Have a quiet drink together (just one!) before you set off for the church. You will of course already have timed your trip from the groom's house to the church, and therefore know when you must leave in order to arrive at the church half an hour before the ceremony is due to begin. Do not be late!

Checklist 9: THE MORNING OF THE WEDDING

☐ Arrange an alarm call the day before

☐ Complete wedding day schedule sheet

Ring groom and check

☐ arrival and departure times

☐ clothes and accessories ready

☐ money

Ring groom and check (cont.)

- [ ] rings
- [ ] licence or certificate of banns from church
- [ ] honeymoon documents
- [ ] honeymoon case and going-away suit
- [ ] arrangements for parking his getaway car at the reception

Ring the chief usher and check:

- [ ] clothes ready
- [ ] arrival times
- [ ] order of service sheets ready
- [ ] buttonholes collected
- [ ] duties

Ring the ushers and check:

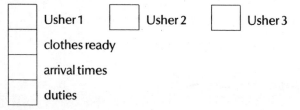

- [ ] Usher 1   [ ] Usher 2   [ ] Usher 3
- [ ] clothes ready
- [ ] arrival times
- [ ] duties

Ring the bride or bride's parents and check:

- [ ] any last minute help needed
- [ ] telegrams will be taken to reception

- [ ] Breakfast
- [ ] Make lunch arrangements

Check car:

- [ ] running well
- [ ] full of petrol
- [ ] clean
- [ ] tie on ribbons

Check clothes and accessories

- [ ]

Pack bag of essentials:

- [ ] phonecard
- [ ] change for the telephone
- [ ] taxi firm numbers
- [ ] prompt cards
- [ ] spare ring
- [ ] handkerchiefs
- [ ] money
- [ ] things to decorate going-away car
- [ ] cleaning up kit for groom
- [ ] umbrellas

Schedule

Time	Action
_____	Get up
_____	Shower, wash hair and dress
_____	Ring groom
_____	Ring ushers
_____	Ring bride
_____	_____
_____	Breakfast
_____	_____
_____	Check car
_____	_____
_____	Check clothes and essentials
_____	_____
_____	Lunch
_____	_____
_____	Leave for groom's house
_____	Dress
_____	Take documents, money and rings from groom
_____	Check essentials
_____	_____
_____	Have a drink
_____	Leave for the church
_____	Arrive at the church

THE CEREMONY

Ceremonies do vary slightly between different churches, but this outline of the wedding service will help you to know what to expect. In all cases, the minister will direct the service and give clear instructions to the participants and to the congregation, so there is really no need to worry.

Your two main duties are to get the groom to the church on time, and to take charge of the rings and produce them at the appropriate moment.

Church of England weddings

Arrival of the groom and best man
You and the groom should arrive at least 15 minutes before the service is due to start, by which time the ushers will already be showing the guests to their seats. You may pay the church fees before the service and hand over the banns certificate from the groom's church, or this may be done afterwards; the minister will have told you what he wants. There is usually a photograph taken of the groom and best man outside the church, but you should not allow eager guests to chat with the groom at this moment. Quite quickly, and certainly before the bride's mother, you should both go in and take your seats in the front pew on the right

hand side of the church. The last guest to take her seat will be the bride's mother, who will be escorted by the chief usher.

Arrival of the bride
The bridesmaids, who will have arrived in the car with the bride's mother, wait in the porch until the bride and her father arrive. One of the ushers should wait by the church door so that he can alert the organist to start playing *Here Comes the Bride*. *After the bride has entered the church he will shut the door so that no one enters and walks down the aisle in the middle of the ceremony. The congregation rise as the wedding procession moves down the aisle to the chancel steps. You and the groom may turn briefly to welcome the bride as she walks down the aisle, and then move forward to stand slightly to the right in front of the steps; you should stand a pace behind and to the right of him. A full procession will be led by the choir, followed by the minister, the bride and her father and the attendants. Alternatively, the choir, if there is one, may be seated and the minister may wait at the chancel steps*

The bride will stop next to the groom on his left, and her father will take a step back. The chief bridesmaid will take her bouquet and lift her veil if she is wearing one. If there are no bridesmaids, she will hand her bouquet to her father, who will pass it to his wife to look after for the ceremony.

The service
The order of service varies, but may open with a

hymn and sometimes a prayer or bible reading before proceeding to the ceremony itself. These details will, of course, have been decided long beforehand, and you can refer to your order-of-service sheet if your mind goes blank.

The minister will say a few words about the significance of marriage and ask first the congregation and then the bride and groom whether there is any lawful reason why they may not marry. He then asks the couple in turn whether they are willing to take the other to be their 'lawful wedded husband/wife' to which they answer, 'I will'.

The minister then asks who gives the bride to be married, and the bride's father takes the bride's right hand in his, and passes it, palm downwards, to the minister who places it in the groom's right hand. The groom then makes his vows. The bride then takes the groom's right hand in her's and makes her vows. The minister will then offer you the open prayer book, on which you place the ring or rings which are blessed and exchanged.

Places during the ceremony
The best man, bridesmaids and bride's father then take their seats. The bride and groom kneel on the chancel steps and the congregation kneel for the blessing.

The bride and groom are then led to the altar by the minister, while the congregation or the choir sing a psalm. This is followed by prayers, the minister's address and finally a hymn.

Places during the ceremony

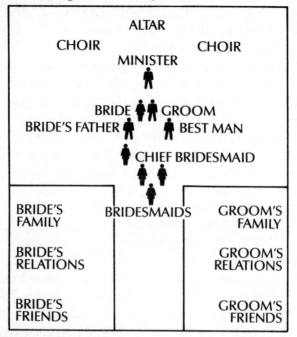

ALTAR
CHOIR   CHOIR
MINISTER

BRIDE   GROOM
BRIDE'S FATHER   BEST MAN
CHIEF BRIDESMAID

BRIDESMAIDS

BRIDE'S FAMILY		GROOM'S FAMILY
BRIDE'S RELATIONS		GROOM'S RELATIONS
BRIDE'S FRIENDS		GROOM'S FRIENDS

Signing the register

The minister then leads the wedding party into the vestry or to a side table for the signing of the register. You should take your hat and gloves, and those of the groom, with you, and pick up the bride's bouquet if no one else has done so. All these will be wanted for the recessional. The order of the procession is:

> bride and groom;
> chief bridesmaid and best man;
> bridesmaids;
> bride's mother and groom's father;
> groom's mother and bride's father.

If in doubt, when escorting a lady you should offer her your left arm so that your sword arm is free to protect her if necessary! Left-handed men should ignore reality and abide by the custom!

The bride and groom and two witnesses sign the register. You and the chief bridesmaid may be asked to sign, or the couple's fathers. There are generally a few photographs, and the chief bridesmaid returns the bride's bouquet. You should make sure that you, the groom and ushers all have your hats and gloves if you are wearing them, before the bells peal and the music sounds for the recessional from the church, which follows in the same order as it entered the vestry.

Settlement of fees

If the minister has asked that the various fees should be paid after the ceremony, it is the best man's job to stay behind in the vestry to settle financial matters while the recession takes place. Payments are made to the clergyman, choir and bell-ringers. The most discreet way of doing this is to put the money (cash or cheque) in envelopes, with the name of the recipient written on the outside.

The photographs

These are generally taken outside the church although if the weather is really dreadful, it might be worth speaking with the bride and the photographer and arranging for him to take one or two outside the church and the remainder indoors at the reception.

Photographs usually take about 20 minutes, and the photographer will have arranged a list of groups with the bride. Make sure you are on the spot when you are needed, and help to chivvy the guests along for their relevant shots, making sure smaller people go to the front and so on. There is generally a lot of gossiping and well-wishing going on, and if you and the ushers can keep things moving it will be much more efficient. Keep a close eye on the clock, bearing in mind the time the reception is due to begin and the time that the church is booked for the following wedding.

Leaving for the reception
When they are ready to leave, escort the bride and groom to their car. Ask the ushers to keep an eye out for confetti-throwers if this is not allowed, and suggest guests keep it for the reception. The bride and groom leave first, followed by the bridesmaids. Next the bride's parents leave, in their own car if it has been left at the church for them before the wedding, followed by the groom's parents in their own car. At larger, more formal weddings, there may be two additional official cars, the first for the bride's mother and the groom's father, the second for the groom's mother and the bride's father. When the wedding party have all left, the other guests follow them to the reception.

You should have organised any necessary lifts beforehand, but double-check that no one will be left stranded. Ask the chief usher to check the church for any property left behind (including top hats and gloves), and be the last to leave. You may drive the bridesmaids, but anyway you should leave as early as possible to be able to help at the reception.

Double weddings

If two couples are getting married at the same service, both grooms will have their own best man, and each will undertake exactly the same duties as if there was a single bridal couple. However, it might be a good idea for them to get together beforehand to sort out the order of precedence and other matters.

The rules of precedence are complicated. If the two brides are sisters, then the elder bride takes precedence, and will walk down the aisle first, followed by her attendants. The younger bride will walk behind the first bride's attendants, with her retinue following her. If the brides are not sisters, the elder bridegroom is assumed to be the senior, and his bride takes precedence. The first bride and her groom will take their vows first and sign the register first. The two best men are jointly responsible for manoeuvring the two wedding parties into position for the photographs, and then each should see his own bridal couple into their car to the reception venue.

If the duties of the two best men do happen to clash, then the senior bridegroom's best man takes priority. For example, if the grooms or brides are related to each other, there will be only one receiving line at the reception.

Catholic weddings

A Catholic wedding service is very similar to the Church of England ceremony, although the couple will require a licence from the superintendent registrar, which you should check has been brought to the ceremony. The priest will almost certainly be authorised to register the marriage, in which case there is no need for a registrar to be present. If both the couple are Catholic, it will probably be a Nuptial Mass, otherwise it will be a simple ceremony.

The pattern of the service covers the significance of marriage, declarations that there are no lawful reasons against the marriage, and that the couple will accept and bring up children within the Roman Catholic faith. The priest asks them to declare their consent to marry, to which they reply, 'I will'. They then exchange vows, and in addition to a ring the groom gives gold and silver to the bride as a token of his worldly goods. When the rings have been blessed, the groom places the ring first on the bride's thumb, then three fingers in turn saying, 'In the name of the Father, the Son and the Holy Ghost. Amen.' The blessing concludes the service, and the wedding party move to the sacristy to make the civil declaration and sign and witness the register.

This is the end of a simple service, but a Nuptial Mass would follow in a full service.

Jewish weddings

For a Jewish wedding, the best man would almost certainly be Jewish and would therefore be familiar with the religious ceremonies and customs. As with other churches, the form of the service does vary. The couple will require a licence from the superintendent registrar, but the Minister or secretary of the synagogue is usually authorised to register the marriage. If he is not, either the registrar must himself be present at the ceremony, or there must be a civil marriage before the religious service.

The ceremony takes place under a chuppah, or canopy, decorated with flowers. In an Orthodox service, the men and women would sit on opposite sides of the synagogue, and in this case both men and women will have their heads covered. The groom is escorted from the door of the synagogue to the chuppah by the male members of his family, who then return to escort the bride, who stands on his right hand side.

The rabbi gives a short address, before the groom places a ring on his bride's right index finger. The couple exchange promises and vows, the rabbi chants the Seven Benedictions, then the couple each sip wine twice from the same glass before the bridegroom breaks the glass beneath his heel. This symbolises that they should share their pleasures and halve their troubles. The broken glass symbolises the weakness of marriage without love. Finally they sign the civil contract, if there was not an earlier civil wedding, and sign the register of the synagogue before two witnesses.

Non-conformist weddings

The service in a non-conformist church may be simpler than the Church of England ceremony, but the best man's duties are the same. The couple require a licence, and a registrar should attend if the minister is not licensed to register the marriage. The exact form of the marriage itself, and the style of the reception, will vary from church to church. You should therefore ask the bride if there are any important points you should be aware of. For example, does the church have a centre aisle; will alcohol be served at the reception; will jokes be acceptable in your speech; will a grace be said before the meal?

Civil weddings

A civil wedding at a registry office is a shorter and less formal affair, and there is less for the best man to do, although he should still make sure that he gets the couple to the office on time, and produce the rings when requested. The guests are likely to be limited to the couple's immediate family and closest friends, since the wedding is short and there is little space available for guests.

The bride and groom will be asked to declare that there is no lawful impediment to their marriage. They then exchange rings if they wish, though there is no legal requirement to do so, and sign the register, with two witnesses other than the officiating registrar.

Although traditionally held in a registry office, civil ceremonies can now take place in some other, more unusual, locations. An Act was passed in 1995 which allows civil weddings to take place in licensed premises, which conform to certain specifications. These, at present, include hotels and historic buildings.

Checklist 10: THE CEREMONY

☐ Go through checklist 9 and make sure you have everything you need

Sequence of events

Arrive at church _____ a.m./p.m.

Photographs

Pay fees

Take seats _____ a.m./p.m.

Stand as bride arrives

Ceremony

Put ring onto open prayer book when offered

After service, escort chief bridesmaid (on left arm) to vestry

Escort chief bridesmaid from church

Help photographer to sort out guests for photographs

Remind ushers to warn confetti-throwers, check church for property left behind and make sure all guests are escorted safely to the reception

Escort bride and groom to car

Drive bridesmaids to reception

THE RECEPTION

You should be among the first to arrive at the reception, along with the bride and groom, of course, plus their parents. Before you forget, ask the bride's and groom's parents, and the hotel reception, for any telegrams. This will give you time to glance through them before the speeches. If either father has forgotten them, find out where they are, borrow his house keys, and send an usher as soon as possible to collect them for you.

Check that the chief bridesmaid has found somewhere suitably cool for the bride's bouquet.

Receiving line

Most receptions have a receiving line. This will consist of the bride's parents - the hosts of the occasion - the groom's parents and the bride and groom. The lady in each couple will receive the guests before her husband. If it is a very formal wedding, you and the chief bridesmaid may join the end of the receiving line and there may be a toastmaster who will announce the names of the guests as they arrive at the door. At a less formal occasion, you may be asked to fulfil the role of toastmaster, but at most weddings you would simply be making sure that people came in in a fairly orderly way, showing them where they can leave their coats and greeting as many as possible by name.

If either of the couple's parents are divorced, the new partners are not generally included in the receiving line. However, the situation should be handled with tact and if all is amicable, the bride and groom can arrange the line as they choose. This may also affect seating and speech arrangements later on. Whatever arrangements have been made, it is particularly important in these slightly awkward situations, that you should know exactly who is who and where each should be directed to sit or stand.

A drink is generally offered to guests after they have been received. You may have waitresses for this, or you and the ushers and bridesmaids may help out.

Inevitably, some guests will arrive with their presents. It is very difficult if the happy couple have to balance these while trying to shake hands, so arrange for the bride to stand in front of a table on which she can place the presents, or ask a bridesmaid or an usher to take them from her and put them somewhere safe for her to open later on.

Once all the guests have been received, you should try to make sure that none of them is burdened with coats or bags, and that they all have a drink.

A schedule for the reception will already have been worked out, and you should therefore know when the guests should take their seats for the meal, timing of speeches and so on. Have a final word with the bride, the bride's mother and the toastmaster to make sure you all agree what is going to happen.

Wedding breakfast

At the agreed time, the toastmaster will ask the guests to take their seats, or if there is no toastmaster the bride and groom will sit down - the signal for the rest of the guests to take their seats. Guide people to the seating plan, and help them to take their seats as quickly as possible.

At most weddings there is a top table for the wedding party. The bride and groom will sit in the middle, he on her right. Other top table guests will be the bride's and groom's parents, plus perhaps step-parents, the minister and his wife and the best man and chief bridesmaid. It is important that men and women should be alternated, and that whoever is proposing the first toast should sit on the bride's left. Arrangements made for the remaining tables should, if at all possible, separate guests who do not get on with one another and seat together people who will enjoy each other's company.

If a minister of religion is present, he must be invited to say grace and should have been approached in advance. If there is no minister present, grace may be said by the bride's father. It is not obligatory these days, but if it is to be said, you must request silence for it.

If the meal is to be served, the bride's father will indicate to the waitresses when they should start serving. If it is a buffet meal, it must be made clear whether people should collect their meal before taking their seats or go to the serving table a few at a time. Check with the bride's father how you can help in the arrangements.

Typical seating arrangement

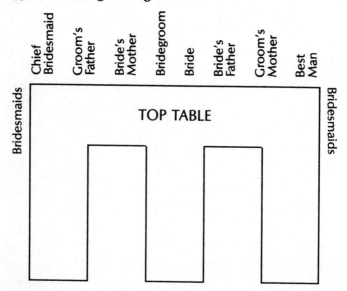

Toasts and speeches

The sequence of speeches and toasts, how to plan your speech, what to say and how to deliver it have been discussed earlier in this book because it is vital that you know all these before you get to the reception. If you have not done any planning in advance, then you could be feeling very nervous at this stage!

As a brief reminder, the bride's father is announced to give his speech and propose the toast to the bride and groom. The groom replies, and proposes the toast to the bridesmaids. The best man replies on their behalf, gives his speech, and reads the telegrams.

You should have your speech plan with you, and as everyone is eating their dessert, run through it to confirm the main points in your mind. Remind yourself how you are going to stand and what you will do with your hands. Try to stay relaxed by breathing deeply and not tensing your muscles. You will already have had a drink which should give you some Dutch courage, but make sure you have not had too many.

After the speeches, the bride and groom will probably cut the cake, amid much well-wishing and congratulations.

If there is to be no further entertainment, the bride and groom will then retire to change into their going-away clothes, while the best man busies himself with their car, luggage and travel documents.

The entertainment

If the reception is to include dancing, this will start as soon as the cake has been cut, or the guests may move to another room for coffee and cake while the tables and chairs are cleared from the dance floor. You can help things along by introducing yourself to guests who look a bit lost, chatting to them, and introducing them to others. Don't worry about approaching strangers because they will all know who you are.

The bride and groom will start the dancing, followed by you and the chief bridesmaid, then the parents of the happy couple and finally the families and guests join in. If you cannot dance, ask the bride what she has chosen for the first dance and suggest that she makes it something easy, like a slow waltz. Get your mum to teach you the basics - there are only three steps so anyone can do that - and warn the chief bridesmaid that you are not an expert and can't turn corners!

During the evening you should dance with all the ladies in the wedding party, including the bride, of course, and as many guests as possible. Be generally helpful in making sure everyone enjoys themselves by serving drinks or guiding the waitresses to people who need serving; chatting and dancing and being generally sociable. At almost every wedding there is someone who tries to monopolise the bride and groom, so keep an eye out for them and rescue the principal couple so that they can circulate as much as possible.

The wedding present display

A display of wedding presents is very much less common than it used to be, but if the couple want one, you may be called upon to assist. If it is to be at the hotel, warn the couple to be careful how open the display is to other hotel guests, since it is an advertisement of the contents of their new home. If it has been arranged at the bride's parents' home, agree a time for the ushers to ferry the guests to the display and back. To be on the safe side, the bride's father should check that his insurance policy covers the valuable addition to the contents of his house.

Decorating the car

It is traditional for the best man to take charge of decorating the bride and groom's going-away car, with help from the younger guests. Make sure you do take charge, and that no one interferes with the car's mechanics, does anything which could be dangerous or could damage the car in any way - even down to using shaving foam on the paint-work.

You should already have your 'decorating kit' ready, and have packed a cleaning up kit in the couple's boot for later use. You can use paper streamers, balloons, cans tied on string to the bumper, Christmas decorations and so on.

Time to leave

Remind the bride and groom when it is time to change ready to leave. Remember that they will also need time to say goodbye to their parents and the guests, and time to tidy up the car, so if they have to be somewhere at a specific time, allow plenty of time to get ready. Make sure that you have the groom's car key, before he goes to change.

Drive the car to the front of the house, or hotel, make sure it is packed with the luggage, and hand over the travel documents and telegrams to the groom if you have been looking after them. Then check that the chief bridesmaid has the bride's bouquet ready for her traditional parting gesture.

You or the bride's father will announce that the couple are about to leave, and many people like to arrange a leave-taking line. Line up the male guests on one side and the female guests on the other, with the parents nearest the door. The bride goes down one line and the groom down the other, thanking the guests and saying goodbye before the bride throws her bouquet and they drive off to the honeymoon.

The clearing up

Depending on how formal the wedding is, you may be expected to help see the guests safely on their way home, and pitch in to help clearing up. At any event, it is polite to offer. Make sure that the bride's mother has collected the presents, the remains of the cake, and the bride's dress. You should take charge of the groom's suit, and can collect a few mementos such as place cards, flowers or napkins either for yourself or to give to the bride and groom.

Finally, treat yourself and the chief bridesmaid to a drink - you have earned it!

Checklist 11: THE RECEPTION

☐ Check that you have the telegrams/telemessages, speech notes and any travel documents that the groom has entrusted to you for his honeymoon.

Sequence of events

Arrive at the reception _____ a.m./p.m.

Receiving line

Drinks

Seat guests for wedding breakfast _____ a.m./p.m.

Wedding breakfast

Speeches — bride's father

              groom

              best man

Cake cutting _____ a.m./p.m.

Dancing — dance with the chief bridesmaid

Be sociable and encourage guests to mix

Wedding present display

Decorate the car

Remind groom of time to leave _____ a.m./p.m.

Arrange farewell line

Departure of bride and groom _____ a.m./p.m.

Departure of guests _____ a.m./p.m.

Clearing up

Collect groom's suit

Have a drink!

AFTER THE WEDDING

Once the wedding day is over, there is very little for the best man to do.

If the suits were hired, return your own suit and the groom's suit in good time. Remind the ushers to return their suits as well, and make sure that they do so.

If the bride and groom have given you a gift, you should write to thank them. Do it straight away even if you know they are on their honeymoon; it will be there when they return and you will not forget.

If the happy couple are away, you may have arranged to check on the security of their flat or house by popping around occasionally. To ensure a perfect end to their honeymoon, take some flowers and a few essential food items round to their house the day before they get back.

So now you can relax, it really was not all that difficult - and I bet you really enjoyed being the perfect best man.

Checklist 12: FINAL DUTIES

☐ Return your own and groom's suit if hired

☐ Make sure ushers' suits are returned

☐ Write thank you letter for gift

☐ Check security of bride and groom's home

☐ Check arrangements for newly-wed couple returning from honeymoon

SAFEGUARDS AND DEALING WITH MISHAPS

The best way to prepare yourself for mishaps is to recogize the problems that may occur and to have contingency plans; a knowledge of the mistakes of others prepares you for such eventualities.

No transport

If the hired car fails to arrive on time, or the groom's car refuses to move or breaks down, you will need to arrange emergency transport by ordering a taxi or using your own vehicle. It is therefore sensible to ensure that your vehicle is in perfect running order and filled with petrol. Carry the details of emergency taxi firms.

Late bride

There may be car problems, unforeseen traffic delays or the chauffeur may have gone to the wrong church! A quick telephone call to the bride's home may provide the reason but if she is en route and travelling in a hired car, you should ring the firm and ask them to contact the driver on the car phone. Meanwhile, ask the organist to play more music and ask the ushers to explain the situation to the guests.

Missing ring!

Rings can be forgotten, mislaid, lost inside the suit or dropped. You should check that the ring is insured and ensure that it is stored in a safe place. A spare ring of nominal value carried in another place, may save momentary embarrassment at the ceremony.

No photographer!

Carry the details of an emergency photographer.

Wheelchair users

If there are wheelchair users, detail the ushers to help with access to buildings.

Babies and young children

At the ceremony, the ushers should seat the guests with babies and young children in the pews nearest the aisle and to the back of the church if possible so that their exit may be quick if the need arises. At the reception, a video or entertainer are good ideas for keeping youngsters occupied.

Lost guests!

Guests are more likely to know the phone number of the bride's parents than yours, so it may be helpful if the bride's parents leave the phone number of the reception venue on their answerphone should anyone get lost en route from the church to the reception.

Lost speech cards!

An extra copy of your speech cards — and the groom's — placed somewhere accessible can prove very useful if the originals disappear from suit pockets.

Speechless!

If the groom is drunk and attempts to make his speech or his nerves render him speechless, you will need to take over his part in the proceedings and improvise by saying something amusing to cover up. You will need to reply to the first toast which was to the bride and groom and toast the bridesmaids.

Drunkenness

A drunken person should be taken to the cloakroom and can be sobered up with water, food and coffee, but if things look serious, phone a doctor.

Disputes

If there is an argument, you should suggest that it takes place outside to minimize disruption, the risk of injury to guests and damage to property. All you can be expected to do is to try to quell the situation.

No entertainment!

If the disk jockey or band fails to show or their equipment refuses to perform, a back-up music system such as a tape recorder and tapes will save the day.

Missing wedding gifts!

If gifts go missing, they may have been stolen; the police and the insurance company will need a list of the items with their value. Stolen cheques can be cancelled by informing the banks immediately.

Need to contact the honeymooners!

Although the bride and groom may like to keep their honeymoon destination a secret, it is sensible for them to leave some details with you in case of emergencies.

WEDDING DAY PROMPT CARDS

There are some tasks which cannot be done before the day of the wedding but which should not be forgotten on the day. This section is designed for you to fill in just before the wedding and contains the absolutely essential information which applies specifically to you and which you will actually need on the day.

You can cut out these pages to slip in your pocket so that you have all the information in a handy form in case your mind goes blank! As you fill them in you can double check that you have done everything listed in earlier, more comprehensive, checklists.

THE DAY'S EVENTS

Time   *Action*

You should have:

        ribbons on car
        clothes and accessories
        money
        phonecard
        change for telephone
        spare ring
        handkerchief
        car decorating kit
        car cleaning kit
        umbrellas
        spare name cards
        spare order of service sheets
        speech cards
        these prompt cards

Car hire firm _____

Telephone _____

Taxi firm _____

Telephone _____

Ensure that going-away car is arranged

Time	*Action*

Ensure that groom's going-away clothes are at the reception venue

Ring the chief usher to check that ushers know their duties, have the buttonholes and order of service sheets

Telephone _____

Ring groom to check that all is well

Ring bride or her parents to offer assistance with any last-minute hitches

Bride's parents, telephone no. _____

Bride's address _____

_____

_____ Leave home to collect groom's car (if not done earlier)

Groom's address _____

_____

_____ Arrive at groom's home

Time	*Action*

You should now have the following additional items:

    licences/banns certificates, etc.
    money for church fees
    rings
    telegrams/telemessages which may have arrived at the groom's home
    car keys
    honeymoon documents:
        passports
        travel tickets
        travellers' cheques

Ensure that cases are packed and loaded

———   Leave groom's home

———   Arrive at church

Church address _____

_____

Minister's name _____

Pay church fees

Oversee that ushers:

    deal with parking
    ensure compliance with photography rules

Time	*Action*

Close family members

Bride's   Groom's

_____

_____

_____

Photographer _____

Telephone _____

Emergency photographer _____

Telephone _____

Have rings in safe but easily accessible place

Ceremony:

> hand over rings when asked
> escort chief bridesmaid to vestry
> sign register if called upon to do so
> escort chief bridesmaid from church

Oversee that ushers ensure compliance with confetti rules

Remind ushers to check the church for anything left behind

Time	*Action*

Oversee that ushers ensure that everyone is escorted safely to the reception venue

Escort bride and groom to car

Reception venue _____

Address _____

_____

Telephone _____

_____ At the reception:

> Take and place guests' coats, join receiving
>   line or announce guests
> Check the wedding present display
> Collect and vet telegrams/telemessages
> Guide guests to the seating plan
> Wedding breakfast
> Speech
> Dance and socialise
> Decorate car

_____ Departure:

> Remind groom to change
> Load luggage
> Ensure that going-away car is at the front
> door
> Announce departure of bride and groom

Time	*Action*

Hand over:
 telegrams/telemessages
 honeymoon documents:
   passports
   travel tickets
   travellers' cheques.
   keys

Arrange farewell line

Collect and take charge of groom's wedding attire

Collect a few mementoes

Check for anything left behind

See guests safely on their way home

Help clear up

——— Venue cleared

SPEECH NOTES

Response
to toasts
_____

_____

_____

Compliments
to bridesmaids
_____

_____

Particular
thanks
_____

_____

Anecdote/
story
_____

_____

Conclusion
_____

_____

_____

Read Telegrams/telemessages

INDEX

Figures in italics refer to checklists.

124